Light relief between grades

Spaß und Entspannung mit leichten Originalstücken für Altsaxophon

Erster Schwierigkeitsgrad

Plaisir et détente avec des pièces originales simples pour saxophone alto

Niveau 1

Pamela Wedgwood

Contents

Foreword

Up-Grade! is a collection of new pieces and duets in a wide variety of styles for alto saxophonists of any age. This book is designed to be especially useful to students who have passed Grade 1 and would like a break before plunging into the syllabus for Grade 2.

Whether you're looking for stimulating material to help bridge the gap between grades, or simply need a bit of light relief, I hope you'll enjoy *Up-Grade!*

Pamela Wedgwood

First published in 2000 by Faber Music Ltd
3 Queen Square London WC1N 3AU
Cover illustration by John Levers
Music set by Jackie Leigh
Printed in England by Caligraving Ltd

ISBN 0-571-52081-2

To buy Faber Music publications or to find out about the full range of titles available please contact your local music retailer or Faber Music sales enquiries:

Faber Music Limited, Burnt Mill, Elizabeth Way, Harlow, CM20 2HX England
Tel: +44 (0)1279 82 89 82 Fax: +44 (0)1279 82 89 83
Email: sales@fabermusic.com www.fabermusic.com

1. Banana Boat Song

In calypso style ♩ = 112

Traditional

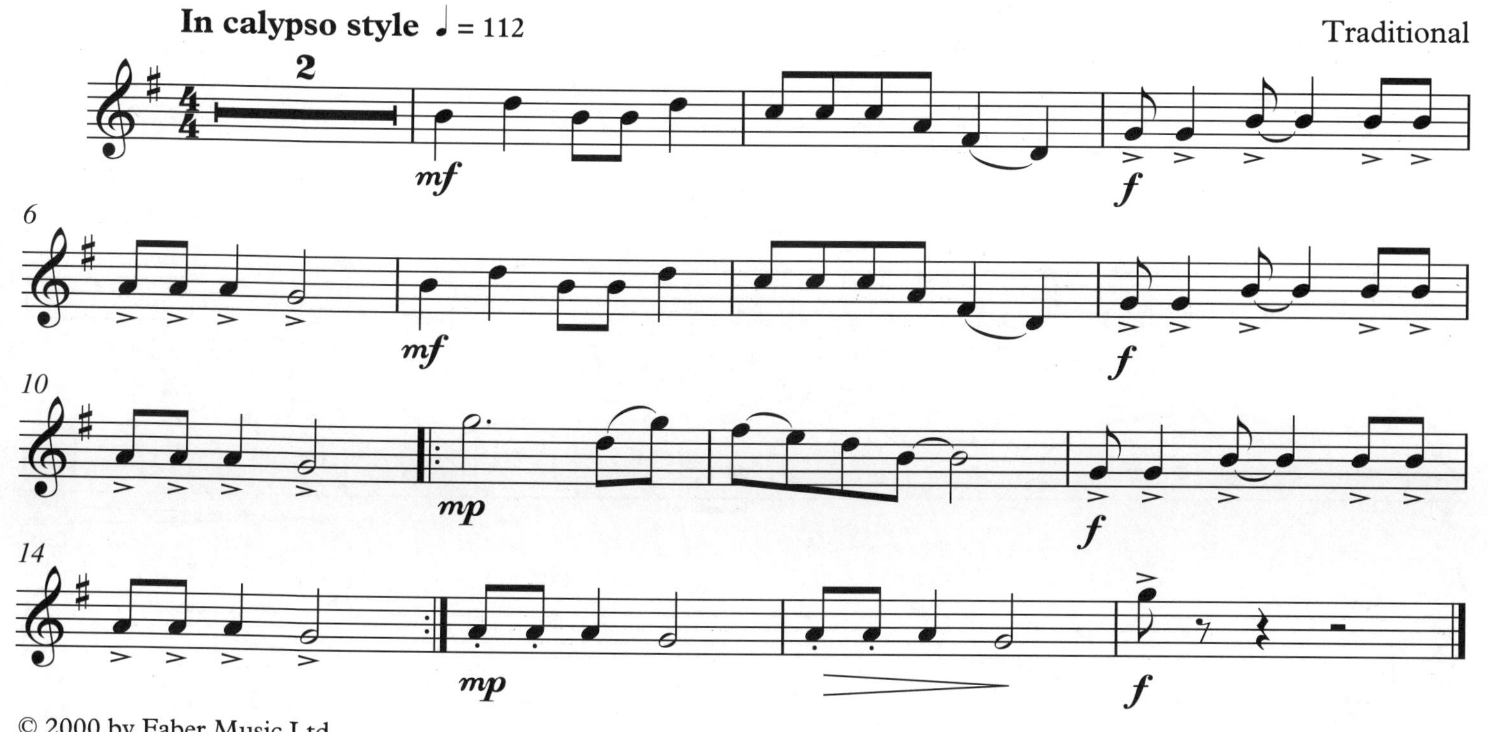

2. Golden Eye

Moderately – with a strong beat ♩ = 120

Pamela Wedgwood

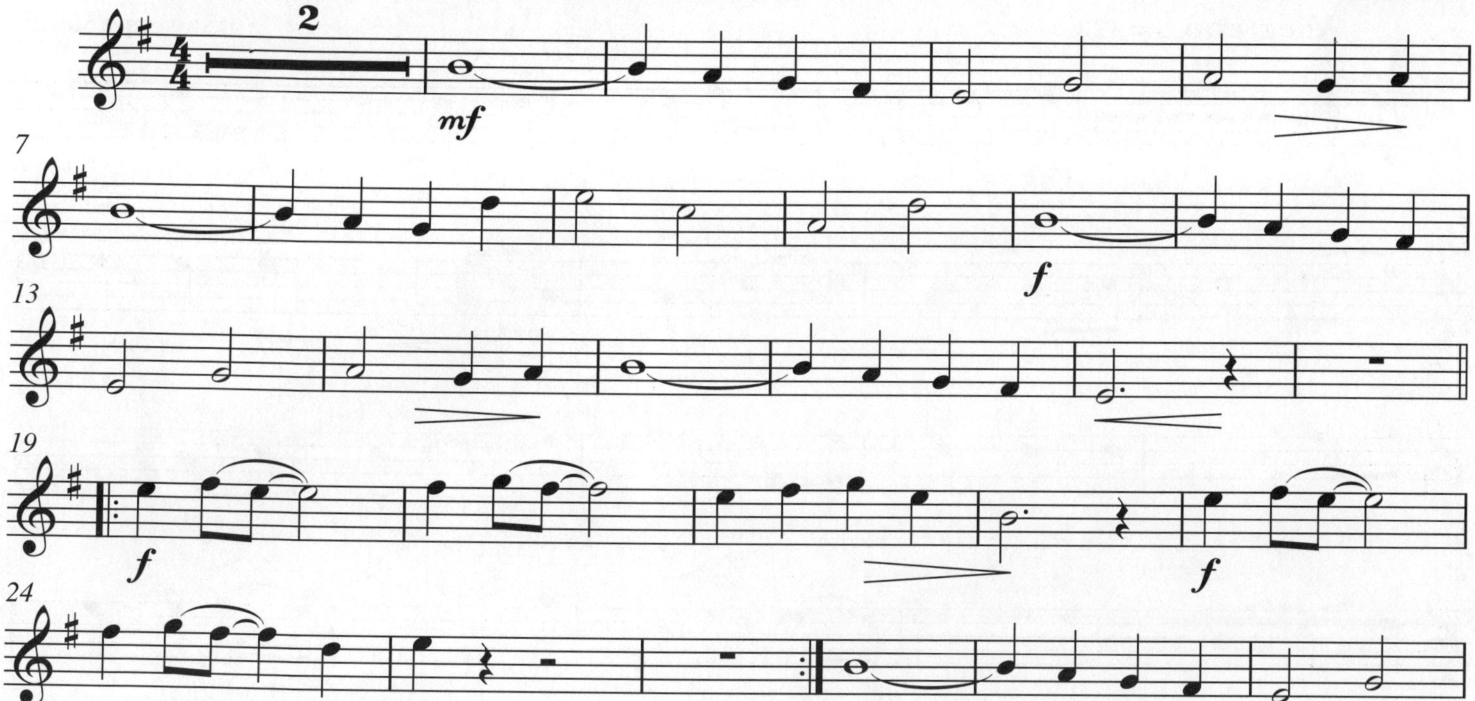

3. Land of Hope and Glory

4. La donna è mobile

Allegretto ♩ = 120

Giuseppe Verdi

2
mp
7
mf
12
17
p
cresc.
22
rit.
f
a tempo
3

5. Coconut Calypso

6. What shall we do with the drunken sailor?

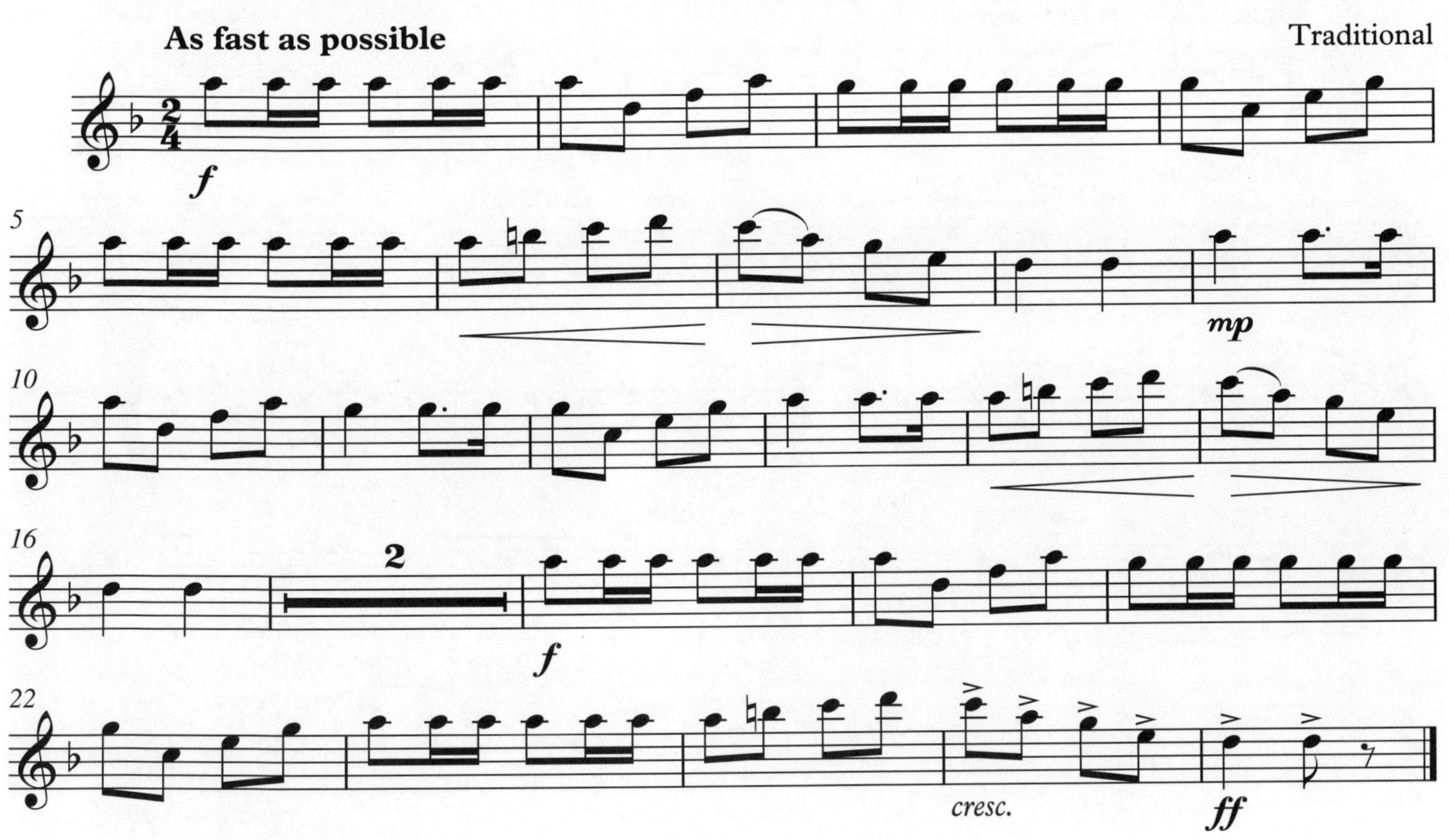

7. I Believe

8. Rosemary and Thyme

Gently – with flavour ♩ = 100

Pamela Wedgwood

p (✓) 7 mp mf 14 20 f mf 26 mp p rall. S pp

9. Greensleeves

attrib. Henry VIII

Gently ♩. = 56

3

mp

S

7

S

11

f

16

f

p

10. Can Can

11. Theme from 'The Teddy Bears' Picnic'

12. Off to the Sun

13. Chinese Take It Away

Moderately – sweet and sour ♩ = 120

Pamela Wedgwood

f
8
mp
f
13
mp
mf
18
1.
3
2.
23
p
f

14. Mr Smarty

Lively ♩ = 126

Pamela Wedgwood

f
6
mp
11
16
Fine
f
mp
21
p
D. 𝄋 al Fine

15. Cat Walk

study in A minor

Pamela Wedgwood

16. It's duet time!

two duets in A minor

Pamela Wedgwood

17. Fandango

duet in F major

Lively dance tempo ♩ = 140

Pamela Wedgwood